AF064572

Kat
Among
the
Tigers

Kat Among
the
Tigers

The University
of Alberta
Press

ath MacLean

Published by

The University of Alberta Press
Ring House 2
Edmonton, Alberta, Canada T6G 2E1

Copyright © 2011 Kath MacLean

LIBRARY AND ARCHIVES CANADA
CATALOGUING IN PUBLICATION

MacLean, Kath [date]
    Kat among the tigers / Kath MacLean.

(Currents, a Canadian literature series)
Poems.
ISBN 978-0-88864-552-4

    I. Title. II. Series: Currents
(Edmonton, Alta.)

PS8575.L427K38 2011   C811'.54
C2010-908138-2

All rights reserved.
First edition, first printing, 2011.
Printed and bound in Canada by Houghton
Boston Printers, Saskatoon, Saskatchewan.
Copyediting by Doug Barbour.

A volume in (*cuRRents*), a Canadian
literature series.
Jonathan Hart, series editor.

No part of this publication may be
produced, stored in a retrieval system, or
transmitted in any forms or by any means,
electronic, mechanical, photocopying,
recording, or otherwise, without the prior
written consent of the copyright owner
or a licence from The Canadian Copyright
Licensing Agency (Access Copyright).
For an Access Copyright licence, visit
www.accesscopyright.ca or call toll free:
1–800–893–5777.

The University of Alberta Press is
committed to protecting our natural
environment. As part of our efforts, this
book is printed on Enviro Paper: it contains
100% post-consumer recycled fibres and is
acid- and chlorine-free.

The University of Alberta Press gratefully
acknowledges the support received for
its publishing program from The Canada
Council for the Arts. The University of
Alberta Press also gratefully acknowledges
the financial support of the Government
of Canada through the Book Publishing
Industry Development Program (BPIDP)
and from the Alberta Foundation for the
Arts for its publishing activities.

She must become simple as we all must learn to be. But I do love her if she tells lies, she also knows more about truth than other people and don't let us see too much the ugly things.

—LETTER TO KOTELIANSKY, OCT 4, 1916.

Clearing the Campground

⋮⋮⋮. FONTAINEBLEAU, JANUARY 1923

I should always try to tell the truth
& keep words I don't believe
in beads of lovely sound.

Come, go; my beloved
who dares kiss a fevered cheek turns
to so & so—

My restless rows, my spotted dreams huff &
puff my purple plume, my pantomime
that sweeps the sands of some forgotten sea, sweeps
the steps where lovers meet too soon,
not soon enough, for the taking of toast & jam & tea.

Bugles blow the spiked woods so violently they cry
& rub & moan & rub the night's skin thin to train-
to-track and back. I cross my poking stick
stubborn for the Heron,
breathless for the finish—

Journals to write, letters to post, fragments—
train-cars, motor-cars—

To review is to sound out loud
& presume the odd word of French—

Here I might imagine Byron, there Oscar by the bed
    or Romeo—(I know, I know)
How to take a flaming sword?
Burn a line of jitter?

Ghosts talk of slumbering soldiers who march from Tipperary
telling one-legged doo-das to any tiger in the street, who fall
fly-fluttering in a milk jug buzz—

I'll not be moved by cigarettes sighing
before their light fades, before they gasp the gleam
from the Hussif's eye. Who scrapes the pots
& pans? Beats time in a teacup? Spots a lung or two?

Jonquils dying in a vase lift their little necks & gaze
at heaven where I shall always tell the truth
slipping between the crack of my half-opened door.

With no one here to meet me, no slender bones, no
wool-warm skin. Spring blows maniac, buries her bud
& time rising from the sea of singing souls
sings too loud for me—

Lovers too tired for talk make boomboom—
rattle; cry out once, twice, then Want wants
everything, wants
nothing at all—

Fire stirs another spark, ignites another breath,
motion, breath, a thousand yous
breathing time's tic tic tic. On the beach a starfish stars
her perfect body, a terrible beauty,
a distant distant dream.

I might stay a while, might—wait
for the rain to rain furiously; wait,
until the fire dies, until
the gleam is long gone from the eye—

Is it God's will keeps me thinking, fluttering,
nervously nattering, packing my suitcase, sorting
my hats & boots? Life's moment-by-moment reverse—
spins the earth, shakes faith in a froth.

Our shadows that point to heaven camp in the cold
confines of the heart where love's anaesthesia surrenders
belly up, open-mouthed, & squints at the body
hurrying, scurrying, not feeling what ought not to be—

O my love, what
to keep? What
to throw out?

I've learned ghosts talk too much
when there is no toast or jam or tea.

Contents

vii Clearing the Campground

Matters Tremendously

2 Boom Boom
3 Matters Tremendously
5 Breath of Time (it means nothing)
7 The Beetle, the Mouse, You, Me
9 J's Pudding
10 Goodbye Soul
12 This Master, This Mistress
14 Their Little Necks Are Broken
16 So and So
18 Little House Upon the Beach
20 Adieu My Darling
23 Stay a while, Stay
24 Wish-wash
26 J Arriving
28 Love's Anaesthesia

~~Rough~~ Notebook

32 because there were no lilacs—
34 Johanna
36 God Takes the Frog's Song—
38 With a Small Sliver of Moon—
40 Softly, gently—

Tired of Tigers

42 Tired of Tigers
45 Pantomime of the Sea
48 The Hedgehog Hides his Prickly Head
50 Doo-Da-Doo-Da
52 When the Aloe Blooms
54 Through the Chestnut Leaves
55 All that is Silent
57 J Arriving II
59 Spring, maniac, maniac
61 Again my darling, Again—
63 The Terrible Silence of Light
65 Let us be tender; let us be kind
67 Where I Lay Down My Head
69 I Would, I Could a Crocodile: Notes for Virginia

75 *Afterword: Kat Among the Tigers*
77 *Acknowledgements*
81 *Note on Sources*

::: Matters Tremendously

Boom Boom

::: MYLOR, SOUTH CORNWALL, AUGUST, 1916

I feel as if I am free suddenly, without warning,
a tree with every leaf turning
towards your slender bones, your wool-warm skin.

Dahlias blossom, lemon verbena stand in a jar
bobbing their pretty heads, winking at tomorrow.

Lacing his boots, adjusting his cap, watching the flames flickering
blue, bayonets slit the night's throat, big-bores *boom boom*
across the sky, somewhere, elsewhere, not here—

Where I can't sleep; it's dark and heaven swells with apples
so small, apples so pale their strawberry hearts beat
the still note of a piano blue, some haunting song a spirit plays

boom boom

Time is temporary; my door is locked.
It may be over in a week, a month, years
in this hollow house, without-a-ghost-of-a-pianner turning
towards your slender bones, your ashen skin;
my strawberry heart beats

boom boom

somewhere, elsewhere, not here—

Matters Tremendously

::: CORNWALL, MAY 1916 | FOR BEATRICE

I would send my soul out shawless and bring you a basket of apples,
or the night soft, suckling the sky, cradling some young life, something
matters tremendously, some *thing* one cries for; once, twice.
I don't know. How many times
do you cry before crying yourself to sleep?

Then maybe the dead might weep, or the fire stirring a spark
might ignite another martyr, might escape the hangman's noose.

I don't know anything about the Irish, or the poor
bride sitting, hands folded across the *Daily* looking
as if passion is about to explode Adam's apple;
love's bomb ticking between her palms...

Even Orpen can't suppress the evening long
or stem the suckling stars, or order the martyrs back—

Who hunts the shooting green;
fires the soul and leaves it waiting by the door?

This little house, this ticking clock, this raging wind
shakes the rounded windows, stirs up dust
without touching, without feeling dry beams press
skin to skin.

Cradling my shawl about my shoulders, I feel the chill knowing
I want everything, every *thing*,
nothing at all—
This—
That—

Matters Tremendously...

Breath of Time
(it means nothing)

::: "THE ELEPHANT," HAMPSTEAD, NOVEMBER, 1918

It won't flower now.
Even if you wish it; lilacs lean against the South
for a breath of time, their small buds blossom,
kick the world mauve and
bruise its tender skin.

I open the window for baby longs
to be kissed and loved from afar where he makes new friends
writing the world thick with love. Clouds burst
and hang dark hoods over the parade and all you see are eyes
the same, exactly the same sad shade of grey.

I suppose it's great nonsense:
life is for fools who gorge on Adam's apple.
We choke and spit; we take more
and more than we can chew and then—
we burst our tender skins.

Still, buried in bud, spring *seems* possible
away from the drunken soldiers who sing
of Tipperary and the long way home.

Is it true that toothless old jaws chomp the bone of yesterday?
(I thought you were beautiful,
today you are the same)
trickler, squirt, drunk, who wrings the sad still song
who sounds the phrase
the sun rises only for a breath of time
It means nothing—

Flowers spoil the garden green where I follow
a labyrinth round and round
choking on cores of apple,
spitting up flesh and seed.
And round and

round
            (it means nothing)
and sleepless,
           (we do not dream)
and speechless
           (the world is very ugly)

And baby wanting kisses
his budding lips, his purple kiss—

Then the dark hood slides over our eyes,
then the same sad shade of grey.

Tell me,
can you tell me Tig,
it is nothing?

The Beetle,
the Mouse, You, Me

::: PARIS, FEBRUARY, 1922

Arranging the chessmen we bump and thump
king against queen: your morning hat, my black cape,
our rags and shreds flutter and blow about from room to room.

With nowhere to hide this storm in my chest
rattles and ebbs, and rattles, and carries
me further to sea where Nothing looks as I remember
Nothing sounds as I remember, this
terrible beauty, this distant, distant dream.

The evening thrusts his head around the door
and waking, I do not know him; I do not
recognize the I, me, she
who makes her way with too little time
between the knight's tired horse dragging its feet,
clip clop, or Mouse padding up the stairs hurry,
scurry, flicking her ringéd tail.

This must be how going out of one's mind feels,
squinting to see beyond the body, to
recognize the gesture: the brow raised,
the flickering fringe of an eyelash, or footsteps
creeping towards me, suppressing desire, not feeling
what ought not to be killed, what ought not to die.

It is foolish to not know you,
dreaming, waking.
You.

The beetle on its back kicks air,
reads the paper upside down, forgets
the contents of a good book and lies
belly up, helpless, gazing out to sea.

Yet Nothing is, Nothing sounds too
tired to check or mate. The fat mouse
licking her lips and chops lays out rags,
flutters about the room and fluffs
this ebb and rattle, bumps this king and queen.

My morning hat, your black cape—

What we ought to know is foolish—
What we ought to know is bruised—

& Nothing

Nothing, is as I remember—

J's pudding

::: ROSE TREE COTTAGE, BUCKINGHAMSHIRE, JANUARY/MARCH 1915

You've got to love me!
The war's horrid and everyone's talking dull and witless.
Sparrows cheep about like chickens,
but the pudding my dear is lovely.

The day folds and narrows news of the War again;
it rains and makes me forget my mud-coated shoes,
my heart-beat-about my chest, for no reason,
for no one at all—

I feel small and frightened of the bugleman, the stoneman
who breaks day in pieces, chisels the afternoon to pistol.
Here we lie sleeping; here we shall rot—
But the pudding my dear is just lovely.

It's funny to sit so quietly, mouth sewn, while he strings out a story
my heart scarcely beats, my knees knock hope's light witless and dull;
the window's splattering rain shoots me here and here—
But the pudding my dear is fine.

Goodbye
Soul

::: CHELSEA, DECEMBER, 1917

Without you, goodbye soul.
There ain't going to be no tea.

Of this Im certain, although I can't tell
just when or where, you, me, each slender wing one-
and-the-same bird, bigger than you, me, together,
the width of its wing greater than our all years, together,
apart. Shall we ever be happy?

The gods ride high pulling my bullied banter, dragging
the sun's cruel chariot back and forth and back until
Day's neck breaks, youth's shadow slumps in a chair.
Bones ache, I lean a little heavier upon my stick;
my chest boils Time's blood black, turns my fingers blue.

I can't go out; I can't stay in where my toes snap and crack and snap
the year in a wishbone—wishing my shaking hand, my battered pen
might beat my plate of fishes, talk sense to the dead—

The morning spent, the fire smokes the grate and burns my saucer of milk,
chars my lions' steak. The Medicine man takes my hand,
strokes it softly, calls me *dear* and stoking my iron-flat,
buries hope beneath blankets, spins desire on a spit
and burns the rest of the year.

I'm done doing nothing, done listening;
the gossips sing *Happy Morn* louder than the kettle's whistle, louder
than my scratching pen; the bird at the window watches
me do nothing, dream nothing, and meeting its eye
wishing you, me, all our years together amount to nothing if—

I want *goodbye* in a teacup.
I want the world to know—

Sitting on the couch, hope lies bigger than the two of us,
more brilliant than the two of us writing this, that,
another review; the *New Age* makes me grind
my teeth, puts my niblick to the test—
And no one makes me tea, no one calms the black bird
flitting before the window, knocking against the glass.

I might answer *hello God*, and reclining on the couch, watch
the soul stretch itself limb to fleshless limb, a wishbone wishing—
I'd sooner snap and crack than ache and dream
two black birds long and slender,
two black birds long and slim.

Goodbye hunches in a teacup,
watches you, me wishing the night thin—
all our years together split
on the spindle of a spin—

This Master, This Mistress

::: CORNWALL, APRIL 1916

Who wants to live like grown up people lost in a world of sex?

Gorse curse among the grey rocks, bluebells bicker;
violets dumb with dialogue endlessly argue the same conclusion.

And all the while the wind whines,
and all the while he sews
sex into sad corners of a witless room.

Walls shake the mouth suckling the seam
of some imagined breast. O, Love looks good
in a pretty hat, tastes a pretty tea—

And all the while he raves and roars
and all the while he beats his fists,
adders curl around his legs, Cupid smokes a fag—

And morning gives itself to afternoon—dark
furl-of-cloud; its ebony rain streams down the window
rivers of hate; how I hate
this master, this mistress pushing each to each.

Id rather die in the middle of a laugh, or scrabbling
into bed, wink my toes before the fire than hear more
of intercourse worming through the heart.

Just now the wind stops speaking.
Just now violets in a frenzy-spatter, natter, begin
to talk of tea & trimming hats.

Rocks spit obscenities upon the suckling sea,
find the shore's withered breast, now each to each
sex recoils an endless end of wrong—

I'd rather die laughing, bound for bed
scrabble in my pyjamas, wink my toes in stone than live
among the grown ups stitching sex, sucking Cupid's stupid fag, or
sniffing tired posies tied with pretty ribbon, bound with pretty string—

The needle darns a pair of trousers, stitches rings
around the sun; who sexes morning, who coils about wild?
Fever breaking, breaks, begins again.

This master, this mistress who wants to live
grown up, sin to sin?

Their Little Necks
Are Broken

::: CHELSEA, JULY 1917

Oh, God dont
lean over the dark like that, afraid.

Fall in or out. Make up your mind;
damnation isn't a place to dilly.

You'll need a cover; some sort of mask
to mask the self exposed, choking, smoking,

pacing about the room. Hardly breathing biff
you rattle a little run-down spit; you cough about the room.

And rising for a moment, to pace before the fire
complain its glow is too hot, not hot enough, complain—

What do you feed your conscience?
Valerian by the bed?

There was a little man…
Dostoevsky's dead.

The day shot, geraniums nod in the vase;
their little necks broken, their little gaze gazed.

And breath trembling, hand reaching for a match
you fan the fan of self contempt burning on a stick:

if they shall kill me,
if I shall die—

Dark blows about uncertainty, smokes
the smouldering match, burns

black to blue and black, rots a pile of tea.
Oh God, this bitter end of bread; this sticky trail of jam.

Shadows forget the sun rises then falls back burning into bed.
Now there's dust in the gloom.

Faith flies at the window fluttering moth balls of self-contempt.
if i shall die, when I am killed...

We bind together weeks, months, unmoneyed years
quiver indecently, indelicately, afraid to be extravagantly frank–

The bread is stale, the milk fouled,
there is no jam for tea.

Don't lean into the dark, afraid.
Their little necks broken, their narrow gaze, gazed.

So and So

::: GRAY, FRANCE, FEBRUARY 1915 | FOR F

We talk so much a whole life passes in an afternoon
already we've been to India, South America, Japan—

This room might be our ocean, far off & nowhere
our rowboat rowing the dark
wave upon wave
waves of you.

We agree to undress slowly, naturally,
to make our way to the bed where love is so
and so; it's hard not to laugh about our kiss,
mumbling, *here and here*
fumbling in the dark.

I'm not afraid curled up in your arms,
your pretty face, your pretty hair, your hand racing past
my blue
red
blue
wave upon wave
waves of you.

We might find happiness in a garden dreaming
rabbits lay great nests of eggs, robins gather honey,
and soldiers lying on the grass search for four-leaf clover—

Life passes in an afternoon; whole and wavy,
red and blue
it's hard to be afraid with you.

In the darkness you are the très paresseux;
(I know, I know)
this old boat, these oars, this wave rising blue.

Already the day rows past the afternoon
mumbling in the dark, stumbling, speaking French, so
and so our love
so and so—

Little House Upon the Beach

::: BANDOL, JANUARY/FEBRUARY 1918

God knows how many Ancient Mariners cry for the bird
or fishermen's wives pacing before a dying fire curse their husbands
and longing for them to come home, curse a little more.

The Mariner's book is full of sand; he never turns the page.

Lungs ache and burn the season sorry,
to complain of windstorm, sandstorm, for the rip
and tug, for palm trees torn limb from limb.

Whose leaf-like hands glisten in the wet
miles away upon the beach?
This maudlin sea rising, falling before noon, or after:

a blooming star, a prickling rose. I'm tired of dark dogs
sniffing along the beach unearthing fever in the sand,
digging at piles of blood and bone and bone.

The Mariner's book is very old, he cannot turn the page.

I'm going grey along the temples; I'm tired of speaking French,
bowing to the butcher, I creep in shawls and coats
wooly for a flower; yesterday smells sweet, sweet—

For the memory of this little house upon the beach.

Last night I wrote my English lip curling against corruption,
I did not speak or follow women tracking every troop
every frock and hat for threads of perfect yesterday.

To bind this little house upon the beach.

I'm getting fat on salad and conversing in the raw *what*
constipates a conversation, *when* space between a comma,
where breath between a bite?

Every word, my remedy for despair,
my every-stop, my rounded little leaf
stretching palm to palm burns across the sand.

The Mariner and his piles of bones,
the fishermen's wives cursing each to each
unhoused, deserted, dogged.

It's work that matters—always, to keep alive this
ache for yesterday—sweet sweet—

For this little life upon the beach.

Adieu
My Darling

::: BUCKINGHAMSHIRE, NOV/DEC. 1914

Adieu my darling, it's been lovely
to find a way between the extreme round of turnips
and the sharp arms of spiked woods
where you hammer my heart, stretch hope
over trees, bleed the moon, and slowly,
steal its glow—

How I hate your reckless abandon;
this hard exterior, this
space where our white skins rub—

Borders fray; feelings tear
you and me
and you,
and you,
chewing at bits of bone.

I'd like to kill my you, your me,
and setting them free in this house, play
among the dust balls beneath the bed.

I'd like to hold hands over our new grave and cry once,
long and hard; forget the gasp of breath,
the lung-spot, you—

With a bit of luck we can say goodbye,
adieu darling it's been lovely
living in the past with my unbuttoned shoe, lying

in bed without blankets, darning the moon's bloodless face,
pulling the needle in/out, drinking your boiled words;
the cup chipped, the kettle dry.

The room folds me over a stiff backed chair, dangles
my feet above the threadbare carpet where your reckless abandon,
your razor arms keep pulling me back.

The fly in the milk jug drowns before noon; we struggle,
sink, surface again, briefly, madly, fluttering
our violent wings snuff out the light.

Flies buzz in a sink of dirty dishes,
the ashtray spills its guts, the fish you haven't skinned lies
where our new grave opens, flickers

for a moment, brilliant and white; the promise of—
the edge of—your penknife flashing
slits my throat, steals my light.

Shadows undress the Morning, and dragging
her foot, catches her heel in the closed curtain; she stumbles
across walls, pokes about on skinny legs, pecks

the backs of our necks with her spiked mouth hating
your reckless abandon, this constant pull and tug
tearing at me and you
and you

filling the space between us with buzzing flies,
smoldering cigarettes and days that linger into noon-hour sad;
we fall back exhausted in a teacup or lie

undetected in the milk jug, between razor arms my heart
hammers your reckless abandon,
you, me,
who pulls the needle in/out—

Stay a while, Stay

::: ISLAND BAY, FEBRUARY, 1907

I might rather be a starfish sprawled out in the sand
than a woman watching the sea spread itself into corners.
Plunging into mist, it disappears, shows itself once
briefly and is gone—

A dream, a dream—I shall not wake, but stay awhile, stay,
until the dark grows tentacles, and pushes sweet sleep
under the sea's skin. Rossetti's blue, Morris' green, the circular swirl
of foam-blown sand, an orange sail drifting—

Breaking bread by the sea, I eat too much jam and wish
waves might sweep all that is natural, all God gives we take
this strange rhythm of surf and sand, the sun's unholy light
burns the sailors' skin, pulls the sea's wet rope down and around
their dark flesh, their thick blue jerseys, their trousers rolled to the knee—

Bending and pulling, time rises from the sea, buries itself
in sand and lies still. Hush, and stay
until the morning, afternoon, and evening
when the great beauty rolls face to face with the sky,
Eyeless to a starry night she takes all God gives—

This sounds paradoxical, but it's true.

Wish-wash

::: PARIS, MAY 1915

I feel quite content to live about this furnished room;
this table, this window, perfect for watching the world go round.

Come, go, I long for love, joy, a house, some money to spend.
You can chide me all you want: *women* like new gloves, sweets,
and a frock that is properly hemmed.

Shoulders stooped, brow furled, we write the morning, swallowing
lunch to scribble the afternoon purple and soupy, sup on biscuits and tea.

A cigarette might speak more than what we say; alone, alone,
we sleep on rolling dreams, we toss about the day.

It rains when I dream of Brontë, bread, milk, the brilliance of an orange.
Blossoms falling from the sky land in my hair, my fingers, my grasping claw
needing: you, love, the life of life.

What's wrong with angels ringing round Botticelli's roof, or
nursemaids hanging children from their ankles in the grass?
Sparrows bathe in basins; pigeons strut and puff their plumes
and peck at bits of bread.

Behind Notre Dame a Chinese woman chases a man's cap in, out of the garden;
where God, stooped, his brow furled, sits on a park bench darning the hole
of *nothing*: sitting, thinking the world of *nothing*—

Is life more like Persephone running towards Averno,
her dress torn, her cockeyed hat, her gloveless hand declining fruit?

She picks at the seedless body, and not speaking, not saying anything
chides the self with bread, a little milk, the brilliance of an orange.

The soup cold, the biscuits stale; the afternoon splurges on an extra cig
rasping, rattling, puffs desperately orange.

Botticelli's angels hang blossoms in the chestnut tree,
(you cannot reach them), or swing the afternoon upside down—

The wind does all it can to toss about a frock, to split a seam or two,
to laugh at God's wish-wash—

Wishing there is no need for tea, I confess:
Women love to be alone adrift before Averno's cave,
mouths filled with water—

(wish wash -
wish wash—)

J Arriving

::: MONTANA-SUR-SIERRE, SEPTEMBER/OCTOBER, 1921

Arriving unexpected a cold gleams
behind the Hussif's eye, flutters
as if to argue the inconvenience of company,
to make your bed to lie in, to
fill the kettle, pour the tea,
find a biscuit in the tin.

Here there is a scarcity of blankets; we shiver
for hours gazing out the window until the foot hurts,
the leg grows numb, my arm aches, and head
in my hands, I dream of somewhere else—

When you arrive unexpected, I think of you
greeting the evening while song birds chant
their wordless tunes welcoming you more and more
than the stories I weave round my head;

A clock grows in the garden, ripens on the vine,
brilliant and lovely, turns its body,
burns its skin, then talks another season,
then fades jasmine in a huff;

they can't stand up, they can't fall down—
yet I'm hopeless for these mountains, breathing
the miracle of days, fetching biscuits from the tin—
Quietly, gently, I've forgotten—

How you pull light from windows,
darken eyes, change the beat of hearts
with a slash of your pen, sit, knees together,
bent over a book stealing fire to light a fag,
demanding the moon sit in her chair, knit-
one-pearl-two white socks for a bloodless foot—

Time burns its ache when the candle's snuffed,
when the arm lifts the teacup one last time
cup to mouth, to saucer, to mouth again
when tongues refusing to wag, trip on balls of wool—

We greet the evening song with chant,
a wordless tune, a birdless gaze—
We bend before the window,
we cower before the moon who sits
in her stiff-backed chair—

Wig and Tig in the parlour,
Wig and Tig on the bed.

Pulling blankets we toss and turn
our inconvenient company shivers the dream,
turns the season sorry—

Quietly, gently—
I've forgotten—

Love's Anaesthesia

::: "THE ELEPHANT," HAMPSTEAD, SEPTEMBER, 1918 | FOR LAWRENCE

We are unthinkably alike you and I.
Our black moods, our pinching eyes, how we see
the room off colour, the chairs too big, too small
to sit quietly; my arm stiff, unused to writing
reaches for the pen, stutters and coughs unfinished
sentences prick the throat, in this place that steals
my senses, this place where ghosts refuse to live.

The fire noisy, flaps like a flag
or a fish, hooked, pulling the line too quickly;
chokes, sputters for breath, denies,
denies, heaven glowing above our heads—

This black mood pulls and tugs
as if it can't decide if
night is something to run to or from
the pen, the knife, the cold touch of your hand;

love's anaesthesia creeps between the cracks of words.
Your letter stains my fingers when I read it
ink spots my palms, disrupts—
lines I live by my thumb and index finger pinching
the sun's reflection: pins, needles, what goes in
must come out broken on the carpet, unfinished
sentences, ragged and ravaged as if

I were Eliot's crab scuttling across the sand—
Before the window fields of flies beat their transparent wings
quiet the impossible music of days spent
asleep, awake, I dream its music makes mush
of my chest—Time stutters, the story grows too
big for my mouth, denies,
denies, this place full of ghosts.

We are unspeakably alike you and I, buzzing
unannounced, a flurry of papers, pages turning
flick flick—thumbs, fingers famous for a fit
of orange, yellow, a blade of blue, the pen scratching—

snuffs out the light, the ceiling, the floor, the chair where
I haven't moved love's anaesthesia burns
in the window, sneaks in after dark, pulls and tugs, as if it can't
decide which sentence to finish, which
thought to follow your cold
hand, to reel in the line—
To tell you again and again, o—

We are so terribly alike.

::: Rough Notebook

::: FRIDAY, NOVEMBER 15, 1907

because there were no lilacs—

~~Of course~~ I knew him by the colour of his skin—legs poised ~~around~~ about the horse, as if beast and man were one—~~posin Body and Soul, the world~~ Watching the train flee across the country a skeleton army of trees inch towards him, a crocodile yawning, someone's garden flashing a petticoat frill—

the train pushing past the old man bullies the air, rais~~inge~~s no more than an eye arching its brow, buffets and blows the spirit—the soul reaching for God's hand—

~~Who is of course denied, catches in the bend of a funeral wise, head tilted, slapped by a horse's twitching tail, drowns~~

A buzz of bush flies, a motor car, a cloud of dust,—~~while~~ the (white) road hangs down its head, ~~hissing~~ spits up gospel, holds out a (dry) tongue, coughs ~~and spews~~ a few choice words ~~against a garden gate~~ and ~~disappears (behind)~~—

~~Turning from cattle refusing to cross the other side,~~ Who snivels, who complains, who prays? ~~To lean out the window,~~ To catch air thrashing in my arms I am posing for a moment—a small child raising my hands over my ears—

~~to silence the rushing air since~~—there were no lilacs to greet him so buttercups raised their arms, sweet arum lily lifted her head ~~(in grace)~~—broom blossom made their way towards him, inching through the grass, ~~tickling their growling bellies~~ before stopping for tea, ~~cups and saucers, soda cake and billys and billys of milk;~~

(we do not want to eat ham sandwiches—(this seems so unceremonious)—how to extract strength from pig?

~~We do not want to eat the valley shivering in blossom.~~

Poised, hands folded (in our laps), we lean against each other watching ~~trails of paper, we cut and burn~~ toi-toi staining the night with their scarlet clumps— ~~we~~ gathering gloom in baskets we listen to the Maoris cry—

e ta, haeremai te kai— ~~the fire cracking the stars open how they spill life on the front steps, or death pooling at the back ripples~~ an amplitude of time (I could send a telegram,)

—I shall say it today and tomorrow mad with November renounce every word translating this new tongue laughing of course at what you call dissolution—

(We did not want ham sandwiches but now long for bread and jam).

::: MONDAY, NOVEMBER 25, 1907

Johanna

It's sad really, no one to admire her but light creeping beneath the
door: ribbons, pearls, a bowl of cream.

And the moment flickering between darkness and dawn

the slow breath of a blade of grass, the flutter of two moths rubbing
their wings against the window pane
    good morning
    good morning

With no one to announce her, her blue shadow slips past
her pinafore, past her plaited hair waving
to no one in particular, waving,
coming, going, her hand, her cigarette
circling about a book of poems ~~exhales~~
Byron, Shelley, Keats—a terrible beauty is born.

O, unhappy words, the lifeless weight of fingers
moving the needle in/out turning
(the page,) her fancy-working the sheets straight, pulling
them taut, taking the dust in droves, arranging flowers, pretty-
pretty—

With no one to admire their beauty or notice the afternoon heaving,
the cat spits up on the carpet: air, fur balls, a sparrow's head.
Time sings its resurrection and steps back into the light.

No one notices her hand shifting paper and pen, that
change of light, slanting a line
~~ants who hurry, scurry over a blade of grass,~~
an army of Maoris creep into morning—
afternoon shadows the pale and steady light,
the wind holding its breath—

It's a shame really, all that beauty ~~coming, going,~~
pulling the morning taut, polishing the heaving sun.
That shift in light beats back ghosts, dusts her fancy broom—
waving circles about the room, resurrects the weightless moment to
moment,
mouth to mouthing
    good morning
(a terrible beauty)

    good morning
        (time's resurrection)
ribbons, pearls
a bowl of cream —

::: WEDNESDAY, NOVEMBER 26, 1907

God Takes the Frog's Song—

To the left the falling rain—to the right the violence of hills
trees whose limbs seem to cut across the horizon—
green—yellow—
(zigzag zigzag)

As if God has taken a knife, a pair of scissors—he cuts fine lines, paints the
cliffs red— ~~(they are bleeding~~
~~hills), and falling down~~ & pokes eye-holes in the ground where white
steam rises & watches us one by one—

By and by the mud volcano blinks.
The road bends round the forest and listens to the earth's (almost) terrible
silence—the most terrible breath
breathing trying-not-to-be-sick—
Breath (that) shakes the rounded sides of a great green lake —
(zigzag zigzag)

manuka blossoms hold up their heads—they will not faint they will not
breathe the thick silence —

By and by God takes the frog's song—
The loneliness of a knife scraping the horizon—until there is nothing to
sing but being alone—
Horses chew their way across the paddock
(zig zig)

between cracks of quiet
rain is an open sore upon the earth's skin.
Bye and bye the black pool drips boiling and filthy.
This useless journey, this long night, this endless rain—
I am hungry and it rains
(zigzag zig—)

::: TUESDAY, DECEMBER 2, 1907

With a Small Sliver of Moon—

In the evening she thought an old man stood on the horizon ~~rugged, knotted with tall pines,~~ grim-faced ~~as if~~ remembering the Maoris, the ancient fighting pah—He watched ~~stone-faced~~ the dead drift to heaven, as if pulled by some imaginary hand—and the dying stretch out slowly in the dirt and grass—The river seemed indifferent rushing about rock—it does ~~did~~ not pause to answer the barking dogs—no! or the people ~~stretched along the fence posts by the hotel~~ watching turkeys running wild ~~upon the lawn~~—Who can remember if ~~they are~~ the lost ~~or found—who who~~ can find heaven in a mist of trees?

Where the willow dips ~~into (the) river, where~~ a manuka tree flowers and drops its blossoms, the paddock full—two grey horses stand against the sky their tired shadows stretching towards an open hand slowly, turn and turning their bodies toward night as if today, tomorrow—the sky ~~slowly, splitting the sky into before, after, this moment~~ splits—the moment—then/now—free—

Climbing (up) the rock, our faces swell hot and orange (light)—a bird, large and widely silent flies on ahead—~~and the sky's nest, and the~~ to the river ~~(talking,)~~ thundering about nothing,—ill-tempered it fidgets against rock, circles and circles, twists about the flower—its sorted mouth so filled with rage it might unlock ~~the sky~~ heaven's door with a small sliver of moon clenched between its teeth, a forgotten axe head—grr!

Our voices lift above the roar—louder and louder we speak only to exclaim—the mist—the river—the noise stretches~~ing out~~ across ~~the~~ night's clean sheets.~~and~~ We burying our nose in pine needles, and exhausted, sleep softly softly among the dead—~~who can remember if they are lost or found?~~

::: TUESDAY/WEDNESDAY, DECEMBER 2 & 3 1907

Softly, gently—

Over the hills to Taupo ~~where~~ we bathe all day my wandering
gypsy and her blistered feet ~~salt away their time~~ dream(ing)
of pine and gum trees swaying by the edge of a lake, cooing—
gently—softly—certain of (their) beauty—

~~In a pool nightsky blue,~~ Here Ruapehu combs (out) his long white
beard (and) lord of us all, ~~(he)~~ towers against a steel sky, lost in a
yellow meadow, squeezed under a cloud—I salt away
time, ~~keep it~~—lock it in this book certain of its beauty—sure
my plumage of words puff a peacock strut—

(this is dreadful, what do I mean?—words/strut/peacock?)

Crossing a bridge the feel of the (white) road through my
boots heel and toe, and heel blistering—wandering towards
the Maoris—squeezing under the sun—where a small child
crouching beneath a tree cries, the sky coos tenderly. The wind
soughing in the trees, lulls the child—for a moment—all is
still—then lord of us all, Ruapehu hangs down his head his hair
spilling over the sky-so-softly-gently—he calls to a lame horse the
way you would a child softly—gently—certain of its beauty—

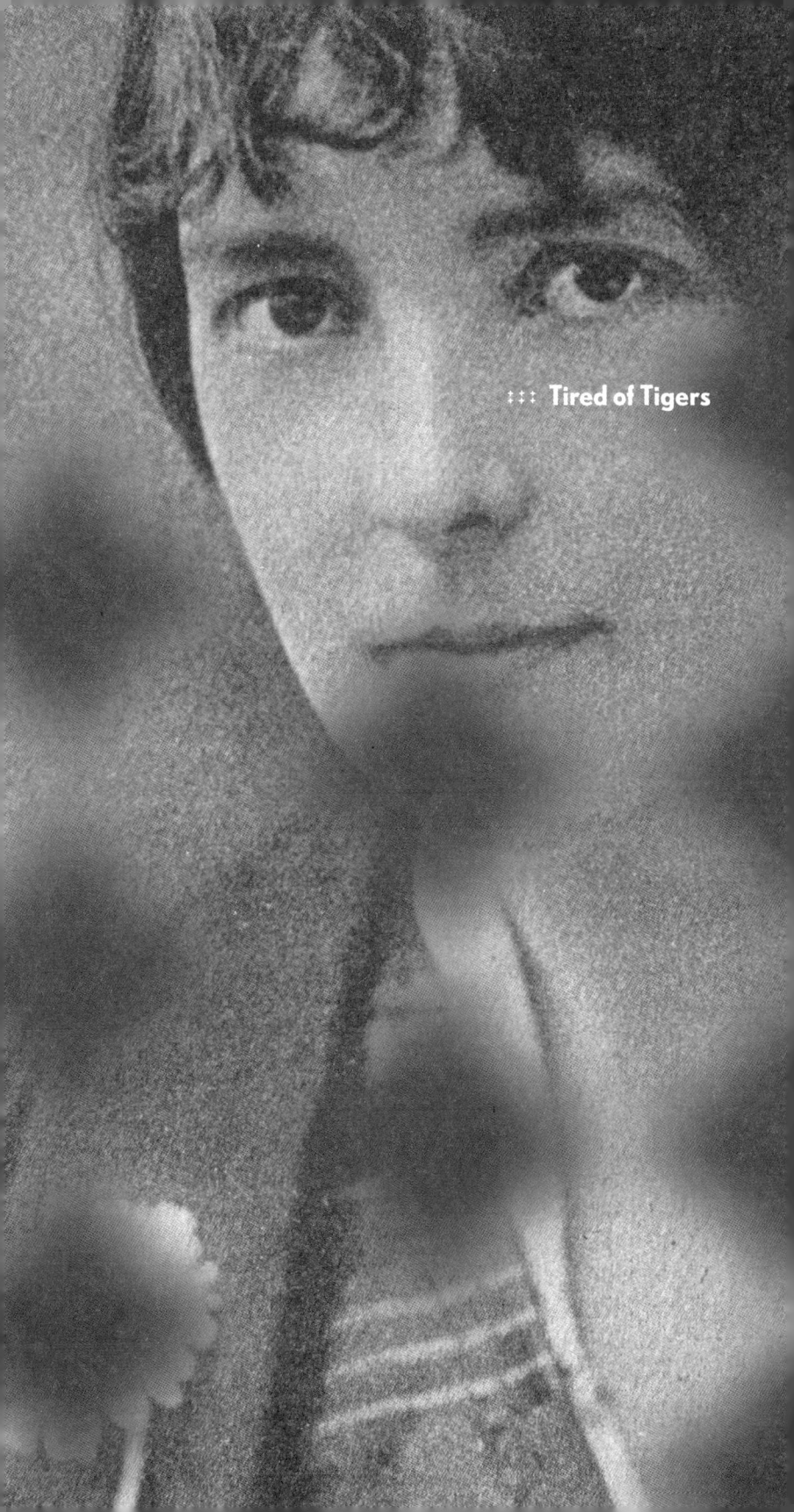

::: **Tired of Tigers**

Tired of Tigers

::: "THE ELEPHANT," HAMPSTEAD, APRIL 1919 | FOR VIRGINIA

One tires of tigers and tails thumping
fashionable accounts of nothing.

Here today, tomorrow I don't speak
wittings of futurity, or recognize
the glowing eyes that follow me room
to room, no matter where I go,—Nothing
takes, no roots set.

Tchekhov was right, my buttons are brass
I salute with a closed fist and suspect everyone
and no one moving toward the latched door, no one
raising a whip to beat these tigers back—

How do you wild the tame?
Start a revolution?
Fire a gun?

The pen drifts and yawns, demands
another cup of tea.

Where does he find these blue-eyed cats
blinking at the light?
Their mewing kittens, their suck of tit
shake my skin, split
my lungs in two
and two
and one

(listen), in my sleep I cough
and cough—
I've lost my grit.

I say nothing
    (I thump about the house)
do nothing
    (I shine the buttons on my coat)
and raise my hand to a useless pen
and scratch for talk and tea.

My mind drifting towards phoneme, drifting
when I arrive, when I get there, penned
will you be waiting with the rest?

Whip in hand, or thumping tail
salute me. My cough and spit
make shiny buttons, but nothing of the room.

Gripping my pen, closing my fist,
or raising a cup in false cheer, I mouth
to mouth the tigers sipping their steaming tea.

Now cats mew in the kitchen and paw the smoking gun.

Trapped among the tame cats, hopelessly out
of fashion, my buttons shine, my brassy fist—
swings against the latch.

I could cough a revolution,
spit and wheeze and whine,
and Nothing might get tired,

and Nothing might get said.

Pantomime of the Sea

::: OSPEDALETTI, ITALY, SEPTEMBER-NOVEMBER, 1919

Stuck on the border of the sea
I brush sand with bound twigs,
and drag my albatross over the shore,
swooch swooch
silence hissing in my chest.

The bird struggles for its last breath, shakes
its legs thin, unfolds its wings to mark its final spot
where death comes slowly, unannounced, here
and *here*.

When I'm sure no one is looking,
when I'm quite alone,
I haul its great body over rocks and heaps of sand
and lift my hat to Charlie
in this pantomime of the sea.

In this pantomime of the sea
the black smudge of my cape blots the hum,
the rise and fall, water marking the spot
where life mews, claws the edge of the horizon,
crawls from a burlap bag.

Stuck on the borders of the shore
I've no intention of drowning, no thoughts
of holding my hissing breath to breath
head full of water, buried beneath sand—
memory shifts my gaze from room to room,
day, night—the hourglass flutters its eye,
the afternoon whispers, weighs on the back of shoulders,
presses cold against the door, and rising
to the ceiling a rainbow: yellow, blue, red
drowns the strange green light—

I've made a life of matchsticks, made light
of shadows so I've no intention of drowning,
sorting life grain by grain to
find the hum of rooms unchanged
my black cape yawning, my pen unmoved—

All the while I think of you
she, me,
someone else—

It's the perfect gesture creeping upon the shore
lifting one's hat to the unholy sun
greeting the mountain's blinking eye
hiss hiss when no one is looking.

When no one is looking, when I'm quite sure
I'm alone shaking this threadbare night
pen dragging its quill across the page, one-legged,
smudges the story, marks the spot—
where my great bird spreads its wings,

unannounced, moment by moment tipping my hat
to a sink full of smoldering cigarettes, matchsticks burning
room to room, dark, then light, this spot
on the lung and its terrible hiss—

And all the time, all
the time I think of you.

The Hedgehog Hides his Prickly Head

::: BANDOL, MARCH, 1916 | FOR F.G.

Ive been hungry dreaming:
English beef, gravy, mash potatoes.
O save me from a salad bowl,
oranges, onions, sweet sentiment—

Ive been wanting the comfort of a chair, to sit
before the fire, to boa-constrict in afterwards
to digest my little mutiny, to lick my little chops.

When really, all Id like to do is buy a pound of butter, or
a book that isn't about Idiots, or acquisitions; love
lists: 5 whorls, 3 engagements, several interminable friendships *and* a Hedgehog

It's all bunkum and Im pure stomach
leaning out the window eating handfuls of Dead Man's bread;
the light changes, the light never the same—

When the hedgehog hides his prickly head.

Under the thick eiderdown I sleep and give myself
to hunger, surrender my longing for beef and biscuits, for
broiled potato-conversation isnt cowcumber, or curdling.

A room full of idiots where dead men feast on onions,
gnaw the bones of Henry James.
(He's dead, or didn't you know?)

Ive been remembering the smell of country,
the birthing of this new self before the War
sitting-pretty–sunnyside-girl from New Zealand
without sense or history, a world of wrong—

People enter the room and cozying before the fire
my boa-constrictor coils round their complaints,
chokes the steady stream of light, stifles change,
never the same, ever the same—

Then the Hedgehog hides his prickly head.

I confess Im pure stomach, English beef and gravy,
sitting on four knobs before the fire, in what they call a chair.
Eating an onion, poking my fingers under the skin on an orange.

An idiot makes lists of things to eat, to sit upon, to acquire
love sniffs the air, removes her bonnet, and smelling your curdling effugion
forgoes hunger, leans out the window to feed leaf by precious leaf.

The Hedgehog lifting his prickly head, the light changing,
the light ever the same—

Doo-Da-Doo-Da

::: PARIS, MARCH 1915

The trumpet sounds, the shutters moan
the sky shrinks a hole in the dark.

I've never seen stars rush through evening like that—
the Ultimate Fish: its flash of fins dives under the night's soft skin.

And the house stretching, rises to its toes, lifts up
its failing arms and scoops life as we've known it, always—

People lean into the black and the Milky Way splaying her legs,
her petticoats rising, her feathered hat, her muff and gloves gone—

Who says Romance is dead? When heads rush, bodies turn each to each
steam rises from the cup, the kettle cries—

the sky calls *doo-da-doo-da*—

In the aftermath, I think of you as a sneak of a pig.
Not writing one ceases to exist among the literati,

their blue swords poke about the fire, picking, flicking,
their lovely tongues full of lovely dreams.

If Romance is dead Jaggle I'm a hatless fool,
muffless, bare-bottomed, fluttering silently across night's soft skin;

the trumpet sounding, the shutter's low moan—
You're a sneak of a pig.

Ash-mouthed, rushing towards the literati
dreaming the lovely, shivering and shawless,

I scoop stars beneath my petticoat and imagine
a flash of fin diving beneath my soft skin.

The trumpet sounds, the dark moans
a few notes here and here a scarcity of words—

doo-da-doo
da-doo da...

When the Aloe Blooms

::: BANDOL, FEBRUARY, 1916

Perhaps the new man will not live.

To speak of the old days, to walk in the garden,
to wait for the aloe to blossom, now, this moment;
there are daisies on the table
a poppy's bowed head.

There are daisies on the table and the sun
rising, breaks the night's gloom, unravels its dark
thread by thread between here
and here and you and me.

Where night rains a halo, a dark hat.
The poppy's bowed head laughs at my imprecision,
my stiff arm, my weightless words laugh
at nothing, nothing at all—

Oh take the day and divide it into four, then six
days of unfinished memory where daisies bow their heads,
and the garden speaks of poppies leaning towards the light—perhaps
perhaps then, this new man will not live.

Memory choosing now, this very minute when
the aloe blooms *nothing* words, *nothing* days, *nothing*
circles about the window, back and forth and back
to you and me, to this new him—

Who nearly remembered bows his head,
and the garden, walking, leans on a stick
snuffs out my cigarette, burns your empty hand
and forces poppies to lean in towards the light.

I've decided this very moment, now—
this new man shall not live.

Through the Chestnut Leaves

::: BAVARIA, JUNE 1909

I must have caught cold beauty in one hand, love in the other
two pair of stockings, two coats, and still shivering
shaking the chestnut leaves I wring out its wet as if
I might make light of the wild woods.

The day refuses to be broken, or narrowed, or shaped deliciously
by small fingers clutching mine—Is it rude
to look for patterns in the pictures of my mind turning
upside down, laughing, falling down on the grass
head full of sweetness—

O Glasgow,
Liverpool,
Carlton Hill—

This side of paradise, my land with no history drifts
slowly, clumsily from memory one season to the next
rain, drought, an explosion of heat.

It's possible it might rain. I might take a little soup, or drink
like a lamb I could crawl back sweet into sleep.
A mug of agony, heart coldness, hand coldness, soul
coldness of sad thoughts I might rein in the morning
with a lit candle, stare at the watch by the bed and before midnight, sensing
morning's arrival, embrace beauty sifting through the chestnut leaves,
laughing, turning patterns in the wild woods.

All that is Silent

::: "THE ELEPHANT," HAMPSTEAD, JUNE 1919

When the coffee is cold, things happen.
Lice feast upon the unpretentious
asleep, awake, the louse & the bedbug suck
my blood, yours, together the we, us
hook and worm our way through your reluctant heart.

Yet, Nothing seems incurable in the afternoon
but the sky, infinite and alone
or the sea crying *Bogey Bogey*
rushing head first into rock
without thinking, feeling, sense—

Where shore meets water, and the waves so very tired,
sleep for a moment, dream on rock
then turning round, swim back again.
The sea sends songs through my bones.
I do not always hear them.

What is here today, tomorrow wears thin
(I can tell where you've stood on the carpet
I know where you pace about the room).

And rather like the lily bending in her vase
neck broken, colour fading fast—
I sense life; feel it here and here
each needle pricks the will awake, to
sleep again, to dream of you.

It's true, I walk a little less.
I scuttle across the sand and leaning on a stick push
all that is silent, all that is true,
all that you—

Pinpricks in the earth might be a way of speaking worm,
to wiggle past the difficult
to climb back in the sand—

All along I've known this scratching itch
this needling jaw unlocked does not speak of love
although I've felt it crawling,
creeping up the neck, a wave of sure,
certainty, a dream—

It's true—I gorge on hope, I hook and worm while
it performs its little trick. Then I stand a little straighter,
then I lean less on the stick and prowl about
the sea shore calling out to you—

The sea might sing more beautifully, might
hit the centre note. Tell me everything;
everything more is silent, everything
more is true.

Bogey, the coffee's cold—
Things happen.

J Arriving II

::: MONTANA-SUR-SIERRE, NOVEMBER/DECEMBER 1921

—time pricks the season,
the sky, the moon, the stars; cold candid peaks
puncture the air, *hiss, hiss.*

And winter's lungs shrink to nothing,
sink to the sediment of night's dull dream,
the sledge of prison, where numbed feet
shuffle the remembered, a deck of cards
no one plays.

You, arch-wallower, acting out yourself,
pruning your plumage, amazed
how you disguise the you,
me, us, the perfect one.

This gesture, like the giving of blankets,
making beds disclaims, pronounces,
exaggerates a thousand times,
a thousand yous working to love
the moment you arrive I am lost
at the window winding a ball of wool.

With nowhere to hide but this cage of dreaming
breath, motion, breath, writhing about the sledge,
arms ache, needles close the book.
Head in my hands, the light gone
fades the you, me, sitting, knees together
or apart, drinking tea & smoking cigs—

Tig & Wig sitting in row
one breath fills a kettle,
one breath pours the tea
one more to snatch a biscuit at the bottom of the tin—

Tig & Wig sitting in a row—

Spring, maniac, maniac

::: OSPEDALETTI, ITALY, JANUARY, 1920

In the morning gulls fly towards the infinite.
We linger in the door, where my heart lies
these secret places, these strange thoughts.

How the jonquil buds and the figs dry their bellies.
A bowl of oranges quietly hold their breath.

Exhausted with tulip-talk, the afternoon unravels
threads of conversation, dulls the senses, witless
the jonquils weak and pale stretch towards the light.

Even the wind has stopped calling, even
the pack of cards folds in the hand; the fire refuses
to smoke or pull the sun back over the clouds.

This pen stumbles and crawls, draws conclusions,
hides the room from the sea's grey light, from you, me,
from this strangeness of being alone, with you, and alone.

The tired jonquil, the dried figs,
the orange peel cries for its forgotten fruit.

Noise boils the air, this day, unable to think, to dream
or write anything more than the jonquil's yellow yawn
tosses about the infinite, mouth open, closed—

The sea sick, the post on strike, the sky searching for gulls,
the Heron and its insufferable roar; my black heart
listens to the drowned who sing the sea.

And nodding to the jonquil, the wizened figs,
the room smells of oranges and burnt wood yawning
spring, maniac, maniac, boils over black.

The watch-glass breaks retracing your steps, lingering
at the door the afternoon crawling, creeping about the garden
my walking stick, my wet shoes, my lungs split in two.

The sky smokes my cigarettes & dreams of ringing bells,
footsteps pause at the door, leaves knock about my knees
then I hear nothing, nothing at all—

But the sea and the wind whose voice breaks
the promise of a crumbled fig, the fumble of a shaking hand
leaning on a walking stick, poking the peel of oranges.

The jonquil nods its pale head, the orange bowl empties
the spring, maniac, maniac—

Where are you?

Again my darling, Again—

::: BUCKINGHAMSHIRE, FEBRUARY 1915

I'd like to know who decides
between letting the morning drain into a chipped cup, or
spilling the night's glow into the sink?

The momentary difference between the cry of the kettle rejoicing
the moment we take tea, smoke a cigarette, work; when
the hard spot in my lung bursts and breaks a little bone.

Snow pricks at the window, pulls the bandage over my eyes; why,
why, do you force your way into the cold and grey
to make it beautiful, to split the flesh?

I'd like to kill my you,
your me, and cry once
hard enough to stop from hanging on the backs of chairs.
I'd like to rest my flouting feet,
skin the fetid fish, once
and forever have it done.

Tell me, is there a God to stop me thinking?
To lift the latch, to close my eyes and for a moment,
see the mingled snow? See—

Moonlight rubs the night thin and the room
in its threadbare dress cries until it breaks
breath in my chest, chokes the you
and me, buries the bone where flies buzz

rubbing the night their restless wings snuff snow's shadow
between the extreme round of turnips, arms
hammering a wooden heart, harden the spot
where my lung burns and bursting
breaks a little bone.

The Terrible Silence of Light

::: "THE ELEPHANT," HAMPSTEAD, DECEMBER 1918

Unlike Shelley's dream where life flowers
from death's garden, here I descend,
back into earth, away
my breath gone, my heart shaken.

I died in this dream.
Where fear clings like the wings of fairies
against the window, winter's frosted tongue sticks
to the glass talking, the wind whining,
until its skin becomes morning's dull grey face.

Its breath gone, its heart shaken.

For this is not the place of mourning.
The sun's arms fold across the bed and walls, where
squares of golden light flicker as if God is stitching a quilt.
He sews my eyes shut,
(the needle prick when it punctures my dream)
then he pulls me back
towards the terrible silence of light.

I will not be lulled
to sleep where Nursery rhymes spin round my head,
wingless, fairies speak to me, no one else listens—
This shaken world, its cold, cold breath.

I died in this dream.

One long terrible shiver and the body breaks
the spirit, the great green glow of self, free at last
rattles the bones, plays me a fool in slumber,
lingers a long while like notes of the organ under the rafters' skin
when light rains down silently, surely,
upon bowed heads.

Do not pray for me. Do not come
carrying violets in your arms, their light
leans out across the bed,
transforms this grey
here, now, all that matters—

I am seeing spots waiting for something to happen—
a hand to reach out,
to write a long, long story
to call it, *Last Words on Life.*

Breathless, shaken, all that matters.

Let us be tender;
let us be kind

::: LONDON, JULY 1918

Gorged on sentiment the piano drinks, leans out
past the creeper-covered windows, past the half-lit dark
and turns a dog's sleep to bark and growl, to beg and sniff.

The world is dreadful when it rains, or doesn't
either you hold out your hand meaning to, or not,
I take my place, speak, or biting my tongue wish to God

I might stop these false starts;
I might rub clean these spots of spotted lung.

In this restless abandon, this rattle, this snap-snap
wind wears words through and through, sniffs and smells
about the gutter, kicks truth in the alley where a dog cowers
about the night, leans against closed curtains, throws back its head
and howls at a moonless moon.

So, let us agree to be tender when the dog barks
to walk in the garden, to talk in bed in this strange light
take tea outside, linger a while over the idea
of nuts and cowslips and fires in the woods.

What is it to be happy, to face the day exquisite
gorging ourselves on words, speaking, or keeping
quiet? Blotting spots of tea?
Silencing the creeper-crawls?

The space to write quiets the flowering star
reduces words to growly-growl, a smoke scream, nuts—
even a dog can't find a lick of meat,
a mutton chop, a scrap of bone.

So let us agree not to make much
of muchness, but instead, to nose about the shadows
when the world is dreadful to rub a spot or two
and lingering in the garden, muse against the light

agree to be tender; agree to be kind.

Where I Lay Down My Head

::: MENTON, FEBRUARY, 1920

The mind I love must have wild places,
a tangled orchard where dark damsons drop,
heavy grass, an overgrown wood, perhaps
a snake or two sliding about my feet.

The mind's love must be immeasurable;
a pool neither too deep, nor too shallow.
I should like to dip my feet in it, slowly,
quickly too: Is the water tepid;
is it cold?

A mind among paths of wildflowers
threaded by God's hand follows no maps, or gardener.
Where fields of Queen Anne's lace spread a bride's veil,
a wave of light this way, that,
gently, and not so gently.

I want what is hidden, not shrubbery, or nails
hammered in my palms, splitting my thumbs in two—
the immeasurable space of sky, a thousand shades,
wind drifting, clearing, clouding
cerulean blue.

I want the afternoon light to frighten my scratching pen,
to itch my skin hot, cold, to wait
for the needling hand to take, retreat
what was said,
what wasn't?
The cigarette stubbed now
the season blooms—

What is it to know the plums' firm flesh
sweet, sour? My mouth a tangle of seasons
knots my tongue and wants love once,
twice—
where I lay down my head, where

I lay down my head
the immeasurable space of living,
writing, not having the strength to write
words slither across the page the very instant love lies
asleep, awake,
I dream of you.

In the heavy grass, in the dark shades of night
spiders creep across my skin and beat out the light.
Faster and faster, then more slowly—
they stomp out the light until maybe
I love the wild place, the unkempt space
between the orchard's damson
and the earth's bruised skin.

I Would, I Could a Crocodile: Notes for Virginia

::: "THE ELEPHANT," HAMPSTEAD, SPRING 1919

...

I would I were a crocodile take an umbrella from the stand
& poke about the dark, & beat
time with his stick.

To fan this wave of dreary, to chill
the heated words & straightening out the pillows
where Lytton lays his head, shake salt
upon the table, strip sheets from the bed.

I wring the idle gossip dry, make puddles on the floor,
& listening for the church bell, stinging for the truth,
pace up & down the dreary hall, then
back and black again.

My boot heels clickedy clickeding,
my teeth rattle & glass, my breaking
thoughts judge the dog dull, the critic silly—
Dilly the hat upon the King, dilly
the horses in the mud.

I poke about the dark & give
love fans to nothing,
wafts to nothing
but stale biscuits in a sour afternoon.

...

How does one renew bliss
when the daffodils huddle in their yellow coats
& arm quivering, spill too much
salt upon the bed?

O, the Vicar says I need to pray but
vindication's sweet.

(I'd rather drink the wine, break the crumbling bread.)

I sit still before a choking fire & snuff
light in my fist, and all the while
my clenching teeth, my rattling gums hum
a stale sad song of self regret—

Then clickedy clickedy my boot heels race
to hurry before the season sets,
I watch daffodils in bloom.

My eyes aren't as good as Dorothy's &
I haven't brought a pen, & in this light
the coughing coughs among the tiger's den.

I long to see a spot of colour, to feel it in the gloom—

To have the strength to lift my arm & beat upon a stick.
(clickedy,
clickedy)

Spring sprung, the coughing talks the mantle sick.

Hours at the window, crippled on my cane
I beat the orange back,
black & blue
& black & black—

...

I might swoon before the curtain
& swear about the heat, then confess
I've been a monkey, swinging limb to limb
devouring Defoe, crying for Babylon—

I put a thousand questions out for tea
(they like it thick, they like it sweet—)
& yet I can't decide if manners boast.
(The tea is ruined when I burn the toast).

I've no patience for the idle, & beat them with my stick
stripe to stripe the same salted-scent-of-self
importance wafts from room to room.

& clickedly click
clickedly click
these tigers must be fed—

so I beat about dark, I cough inside my head.

...

I don't give a fig
to fluff pillows, or sweep sweet crumbs of bread,
or snuff the sparrow's song,
then slump back into bed.

Daffodils dance before the window one moment more, one less
then fall upon their knees to burn their brilliance in the grass.

The vicar says I need to pray.

...

The Vicar says I must forget
I were a crocodile,
(& beat about a stick, & cough upon the dreary)
& salt the tigers' tired tongues—

My teeth ache
    (I spew indecision)
my lungs sting
    (I thump the bell for truth)

& taking the umbrella
hold it by its tip—
pick the lock that locks this cage
coughing in my chest—

The world swoons among the daffodils—

...

I would, I could a crocodile
(clickedly click click)
walk the same ridiculous path, rattle
the same glass teeth—fluff
a pillow where Lytton lays his head, shake
the salt of discontent.

My sad stale song, my little cough
coughs among the tigers, wafts the same self-scent
one moment more, one less tic tic—

The vicar says I must forgive.

Addio

                                                                K.M.

Kat Among the Tigers
::: (1888–1923)

KATHERINE MANSFIELD'S LIFE *feels* like fiction, but I remind myself as I write these poems she isn't a character; she and her world were quite real. The decadence of the 1890s, the excited buzz at the end of the century as the world prepared to embrace Modernism, the years leading to the Great War, the War itself and the devastation following it, and finally, the brief time Katherine lived in the 1920s, are thrilling years in history. Surrounding herself with some of society's most colourful and important leaders, writers, and artists such as D. H. Lawrence, Virginia Woolf, T. S. Eliot, Bertrand Russell, Lytton Strachey, and other members of the Garsington crowd, Clive Bell, S. S. Koteliansky, writers from the *New Age*, *Rhythm* (later the *Blue Review*) and *Athenaeum* including Frank Swinnerton and Rupert Brooke, visual artists Anne Estelle Rice and Dorothy Brett, socialite Lady Ottoline Morrell, and Countess Elizabeth Russell, it is Katherine's story, her endless love for her husband John Middleton Murry and her will to write that continue to fascinate me. Insisting her stories remain "naked," or untouched by censors wishing to force their form or content, she let her characters speak their minds and in so doing declare themselves spokespeople for her world and time. Katherine, it seemed, was determined to leave her mark on the world.

Personal accounts of Katherine are quite striking and inconsistent. To some she was self-centred, selfish, spoiled and insensitive, but to others, she was daring, dynamic, loving, and a brilliant young wit. Her tireless energy to embrace life, to love when and whoever she wanted, but mostly to stand by her beloved John, and to give herself to writing so completely first attracted me to her and to her story. Although by all accounts she became a "fallen woman" in her day, her story begins with the spoiled rich girl leaving home for the perils of the literary world only to find her reputation go to seed. Here, however, any clichéd tale of the woman writer ends. Katherine's life doesn't end well, doesn't sort itself out neatly or quietly and, concluding far too soon, is changed, adapted, and pruned by selective editing, first by her husband, John Middleton Murry, and then by biographers and critics mistaking Murry's truths for Katherine's. Not until Murry's death over thirty years after Katherine's, is she finally able to raise her own voice above a chorus of academics and literary critics to tell her own tale.

In her journals and letters, Katherine quickly takes on flesh. Her heart beats quickly as she loves, leaves, reunites, and is all but abandoned by her beloved John. Sentences are punctuated with her rattle and cough; phrases burn with her fever. The world slants as she leans upon her walking stick to stroll out by the sea, or winces in pain when she moves her arm across a sheet of paper. To write, to record the stories living in her head with urgency and tremendous energy for someone so very ill, astounds, humbles, and inspires me to try to do as much.

To say I have come to know Katherine through words—hers and those written by people who knew her—would be misleading. Her recollections and correspondence show me a woman of great complexity, a woman of many selves or guises. As she once said, we are who we choose to be, but with so many Katherines to choose from, just who then is she?

I hope this little book helps sort that out.

KM

Acknowledgements

THIS BOOK HAS BEEN A LONG TIME COMING & arrived all in a breathless huff & puff quite by accident at the Rutherford Library at the U of A while I was looking for a book by Robert Frost. Whatever was Katherine Mansfield's journal doing in the American lit section? I'm grateful, however, that it was & that I slipped it into the pile of books I was checking out. To this day I don't know why I did—perhaps it was Katherine living one of her lives & stepping into mine just then that persuaded me to do it. I'll never know, but I thank her for this book—for sharing her life in her letters & journals & stories & for feeling always as if she were with me pushing me to finish this little manuscript.

But there are others too I want to thank: members of the Katherine Mansfield Society (KMS) have been supportive by publishing some of these poems in their scholarly journal, but also for listening to me in Menton during their annual conference in 2009. Thanks for her continued correspondence & interest in the project to Dr. Gerri Kimber, Deputy-Chair of the KMS, Sue Reid for her encouraging words after my presentation, and to Janine Renshaw-Beauchamp, Katherine's great niece, whose tears after I'd read from this manuscript showed me I'd got Katherine right & properly humanized her. Janine's personal reaction & response to these poems meant the world to me; I no longer felt as if I were writing a character's life, but instead, giving flesh to old bones. Thanks also to Mansfield scholar superstars C.K. Stead and Vincent O'Sullivan (also of the KMS) whose voluminous editions of Mansfield's letters & journals I used in the making of these poems. That O'Sullivan sought me out in Menton in a sea of Mansfield scholars & encouraged me to publish this collection also helped assure me I had captured not only the writer we had come together to celebrate, but the woman as well.

 I also travelled to several retreats with this manuscript and wish to thank a number of people who gave up their time to discuss these poems over the years or help me settle into this work: Tena & Rudy Wiebe at Strawberry Creek (several times), Brenda & Sheryl also at Strawberry Creek for feeding & watering me so very well, Daphne Marlatt at Sage Hill for helping me realize I wasn't done yet (& oh how I wanted to be), for listening to my ideas on shaping the manuscript, & for believing enough in the book to recommend it to others. Thanks to the circle of writers I met at St. Peter's in the summer of 2009 where I finished editing the manuscript & where I first met novelist Sandra Campbell who shared with me her experiences marrying into the Canadian branch of the Beauchamp family. What a wild story that was & how very grateful I am to her for sharing her tales with me over several Indian dinners in Toronto & walks around the wet cornfields during our retreat. She truly helped make Katherine feel alive for me. Barbara Scott also gave generously of her time during the Writers Guild of Alberta's Banff retreat in 2008 when we were both so ill & made me rethink some of the wacky grammar I was using. Thanks for Mitch Kowalski at the Toronto Writers' Centre for getting me a spot to write when it was still in the heart of Yorkville. How many glorious afternoons I spent editing my work on that balcony! I wrote so many of these poems there & accomplished a great deal. Also & always thanks to my forever mentor, Doug Barbour, who heard me read some of these poems ages ago at the Poetry Festival in Edmonton & told me to stop researching K's life & get on with writing the poems–how very right he was & how he has always pushed me towards a finish! His editing advice was also a godsend when my brain was beyond being frazzled & I really needed him. Peter Midgley's enthusiasm for the manuscript at U of A Press is also noteworthy–his quick response, coming no less than an hour after I dropped it off at his office, gave me the courage to hope this would quickly fly—& after a long & difficult road, how very much I welcomed that. Also thanks to Jeff Carpenter at the press for his continual interest in my work & for reminding me over & over again to send this manuscript in when I'd finally completed it. A push is always useful.

   So too is the help one receives from one's writing group: Alice Major, Jenna Butler, Jannie Edwards and Catherine Owen. Their willingness to listen to my queries was instrumental in shaping some of these poems. I also wish to thank Lane Arndt who has recently begun writing music to accompany "Doo-Da-Doo-Da" and Marie-Pierre Castonguay & Ross Bragg of Oops! Design who are working on the accompanying videopoem. Dorian Bibbey at Dorian Design also has designed a wonderful image to promote this book on my web page. Compilations are brilliant & I am most grateful & humbled to know & to work with so many talented artists.

   Not to be forgotten are those closest to me who had to live with this book & me rattling on about it until I was finished. Without the help of any grants I ranted & raved & fumed an awful lot. My mother listened patiently & her fine ear for language & rhythm helped me to examine the authenticity of K's voice. As well, my mother's comments on many of the early drafts I wrote in Toronto were invaluable. Forever questioning my intent & reasons for writing about K–someone she didn't think she liked very much–helped me to focus & remember just what it was I found so important about this project. Thanks too to my good friend Kate Werkman whose support towards the end of this project has ground me, & to Tim Thompson, who took me to Menton, found me a hotel room with a view to the Mediterranean, & even came to my presentation despite the mind-blowing heat. He also took me to K's grave where I said goodbye & where I realized she had become more than a character, more than the narrator of these poems—K had become a close friend. I'm grateful Tim didn't laugh at me when I cried on the train in France or insisted on finding just the right flower for K's grave & couldn't for the life of me decide what that might be. Hard as it was to leave K in Fontainebleau, it was harder still to realize she was gone for good.

    With the exception of "Love's Anaesthesia" (*Arms Like Ladders: The Eloquent She*, League of Canadian Poets, 2007), "Their Little Necks Are Broken," (which received honourable mention in 2008 WFNB *Literary Competition*), "Where I Lay Down My Head" (shortlisted for *Vallum's Poetry Prize*, 2005), "So and So" (CV2 v.32.2 2009), "Doo-Da-Doo-Da" (*Katherine Mansfield Journal* Vol. 1, 2009), & "This Master, This Mistress" (*Toronto Writer's Quarterly* Vol. 5, 2010) few of these poems have been previously published.

Note on Sources

The following sources were most helpful:

Alpers, Anthony. *The Life of Katherine Mansfield*. Harmondsworth: Penguin, 1982.
Boddy, Gillian. *Katherine Mansfield: The Woman and The Writer*. Ringwood, Australia: Penguin, 1988.
Murry, John Middleton, ed. *Journal of Katherine Mansfield*. London: Constable & Co. 1954.
O'Sullivan, Vincent and Margaret Scott, ed. *The Collected Letters of Katherine Mansfield*. Vols. 1, 2, and 3. Oxford: Clarendon P, 1984–1987.
Stead, C.K., ed. *The Letters and Journals of Katherine Mansfield: A Selection*. London: Penguin, 1977/1988.

The epigraph is from K herself in a letter to Koteliansky, October 4, 1916 describing her feelings towards Frieda Lawrence. Like Alpers, who chooses to end his book with this quotation, I also think it a fitting beginning (390). This quote may also be found in E.W. Tedlock Jr.'s book on Frieda Lawrence, *The Memories and Correspondence*.